Selections from the
Talmud

arranged and with an introduction

by

Barry A. Marks

Templegate Publishers

Springfield, Illinois

The Public Library Series

Old Times on the Mississippi
Mark Twain

Selections from the Koran

Cautionary Verses
Hilaire Belloc

Selections from the Talmud

The Autobiography and
Selected Writings of
Abraham Lincoln

Templegate Publishers
302 East Adams Street
Springfield, IL 62701
217-522-3353
www.templegate.com

ISBN 0-87243-230-0
Library of Congress Catalog Card
Number: 97-60835

Cover design: David Brodsky

This book was manufactured in
the United States of America.

Contents

Introduction

In the four thousand year history of the Jewish people a number of watershed dates stand out, pivotal events that led to vast changes in the way Jews lived and the manner in which they practiced their faith. One such date was 70 CE,[1] when the Temple in Jerusalem was destroyed by Roman legions. Jewish political power and independence came to an end. Many Jews were carried away from the Land of Israel as slaves; others left in search of more favorable living conditions. Jewish communities in the Diaspora grew in numbers and significance and came to rival and sometimes overshadow Israel as centers of Jewish life and creativity. Judaism was transformed in the process. The sacrificial cult of the Temple gave way to a Judaism focused on prayer, ritual observance, and study of religious texts. Rabbis, the repositories and interpreters of Torah (God's teachings), replaced priests as the religious leaders of the community. And out of the welter of Jewish sects and political factions that had existed in Second Temple times, only the Pharisees would leave their imprint on the people's subsequent history.

This transformation is intimately bound up with the evolution of the Talmud, a development that occupied the greater part of a millennium, and with the values, ideas, doctrines, and laws contained in that work. From the time in the 6th and 5th centuries BCE, when Jews, with the permission of the Persian monarchy, returned to Judea from their exile in Babylonia, rebuilt the Temple, and established the Torah, the five books of Moses, as the fundamental law of the community, the interpretation and elucidation of the sacred writings and their application to the circumstances of each generation played a major role in the people's religious life.

Even a cursory reading of the Torah reveals the need for amplification and interpretation. A few examples will suffice. The Torah commands the Israelites to rest on the Sabbath and to do no manner of work on that day but doesn't specify what constitutes forbidden labor. Eating of meat in a non-sacramental context is permitted, provided that the animal is slaughtered "as I (God) have commanded thee" (Deut. xii, 21), but nowhere in the Torah do we find the substance of that command spelled out. The Torah mentions in passing the institutions of marriage and divorce but doesn't indicate how a marriage becomes legally valid or what the grounds are for its dissolution.

During the latter days of the Second Temple, Judaism was by no means monolithic in either doctrine or practice.

The Sadducees, who represented the Temple priests and the aristocracy, favored a literal approach to the words of the Scripture, while the Pharisees advanced freer and more liberal interpretations of the Torah, interpretations that they claimed were based on traditions going back to Moses himself. For at Mount Sinai, according to the Pharisees, God had transmitted to Moses not only the Written Torah (the books of Genesis through Deuteronomy) but also the Oral Torah, an authoritative interpretation of the written Scriptures that was to be handed down from one generation to the next solely by word of mouth. The taboo against putting the oral traditions in writing persisted for many years, but the process of interpretation allowed the Torah to develop into a comprehensive code of religious practice, capable of being applied to the changing circumstances and conditions of each generation.

Eventually, as the Oral Torah grew and proliferated over the course of time, some teachers began writing down notes for their own private use. The destruction of the Temple, the dispersion of Jewry, and the failure of the second Jewish Revolt against Rome (132 to 135 CE) aroused the fear that this material might be lost unless it was systematized, committed to writing, and made available to students of Torah. As a result, during the latter half of the second century CE, Rabbi Judah ha-Nasi (the Prince or Patriarch), the religious leader of the Jewish community in the land of Israel, published the Mishna (the word is derived from a root that denotes "teaching through repetition"), a compendium of all of the oral teachings that had been transmitted over the course of the centuries down to his own time.

Written in an elegant literary Hebrew, at a time when Aramaic (a cognate but different Semitic language) was the spoken tongue of the people, the Mishna is arranged in six orders, as follows:

Zera'im (Seeds)	laws pertaining to agriculture (e.g., leaving the corner of the field to the poor, Sabbatical year, tithing of crops)
Mo'ed (Appointed Times)	laws pertaining to the festivals of the Jewish year
Nashim (Women)	laws of marriage and divorce
Nezikin (Damages)	criminal and civil law and procedure (including property, torts, contracts)
Kodashim (Holy Things)	laws pertaining to sacrificial offerings
Tohorot (Purities)	laws of ritual purity and impurity

The orders of the Mishna are divided into tractates, sixty-three in all, each dealing with a distinct topic or subject area of Jewish law. Mo'ed, for example, the second order of the Mishna, consists of twelve tractates, with most of the festivals of the Jewish year having a separate tractate devoted to their observance. A citation from the Mishna refers to the tractate and to the chapter and paragraph within the tractate where a text is found.

The Mishna might be characterized as a statute book for the observant Jew, but there are a number of features that make it a most unusual collection of laws. Much of the material found in the Mishna was no longer applicable at the time of its publication. Sacrificial offerings had not been brought since the destruction of the Temple a century earlier, and the laws of purity and impurity had, for the most part, lapsed as well. Observance of the agricultural laws was incumbent only on Jews residing in the land of Israel and not upon the Jewish communities of the Diaspora. Moreover, in reference to a given point of law, the Mishna might contain several divergent opinions cited in the name of different rabbinic authorities (those quoted in the Mishna are called Tanna'im). As much as it is a law book, the Mishna is a textbook of Jewish teachings, a way of perceiving, structuring, and relating to day to day reality so as to attain an ideal of holiness (even if some of the details could not be implemented in practice for the time being).

Over the course of the next three or four centuries, Judah's Mishna served as a curriculum of study at the yeshivot or academies of Jewish learning in the land of Israel and in Babylonia (the area between the Tigris and Euphrates rivers, located in what is today Iraq). Teachers and students carefully analyzed the text of the Mishna, seeking to relate the laws they found there to chapter and verse in the Scriptures, to understand the rationale for different opinions about a given matter, and to explore the limits of when a law did and did not apply. If a teaching attributed to a particular Tanna contradicted what he taught elsewhere in the Mishna, they attempted to explain and reconcile the divergence. And they dealt, as well, with questions of language and literary structure in the Mishna (why does the text deal with matters in the particular order that it does? why does it give two examples to illustrate a particular law, when one would do?).

The record of the discussions and debates that took place at these academies is referred to as Gemara. The Mishna and the Gemara together constitute the Talmud; however, since there are two redactions of Gemara, one emanating from the academies of the land of Israel (approximately fifth century CE)

and one from the Babylonian academies
a century or so later, there are actually
two Talmuds. Both the Talmud of the
land of Israel (known also as the Palestinian or Jerusalem Talmud) and the
Babylonian Talmud lack Gemara for a
substantial number of the tractates of the
Mishna (some tractates that have Gemara in the Palestinian Talmud lack it in
the Babylonian and vice versa); either
the particular subjects weren't studied in
depth, because the laws weren't applicable, or the material was simply lost. The
language of both the Gemara of Babylonia and that of the land of Israel is
Aramaic, and the teachers who are cited
there are known as Amora'im. The
Babylonian Talmud is far larger than the

23

Palestinian (a set consists of some twenty or more folio volumes) and, for various historical reasons, it has been the more widely studied and the more authoritative of the two. It is printed with the text of Mishna and Gemara in the center column and commentaries surrounding it on the left and right margins. Since all recent editions of the Talmud have the same arrangement of words on the page, the Gemara is cited by page number and side (one number is used for both sides of a leaf; the left hand side is side a, and the right hand side is b).

The Talmud's predominant interest is in matters of religious law, but since it is a record of academic discussions, the style is rambling and, frequently, inconclusive. Legal analysis and argumentation are often interrupted by storytelling, theological and philosophical comments, Scriptural interpretation, and observations pertaining to health and medicine, the world of nature, or the general human condition. Discussions of law are referred to as Halacha (from the Hebrew root meaning "to walk"), while non-legal material in the Talmud and in Rabbinic literature in general is called Aggada (the root means "to tell"). As the rabbis themselves were aware, Aggada had a strong appeal for the masses, whereas the study of Halacha requires greater powers of concentration and intellect.

Following its redaction, the Talmud was the basis for several subsequent developments in the realm of Jewish intellectual activity. Commentators sought to explain obscure passages and provide assistance for the students of their day, who lacked familiarity with the day to day life of Talmudic times. Moreover, the Talmud's cryptic style sometimes makes it difficult to follow the course of an argument without the help of a commentary to clarify the implications of a word or phrase. Codifiers attempted to sift through the mass of Talmudic analysis and discussion in order to present the whole body of Jewish law in an orderly and accessible manner for the convenience of the observant Jew.

The Talmud was and continues to be a major part of the curriculum of study for those preparing for the rabbinate. During the Middle Ages, when Jews in many areas enjoyed a semi-autonomous status, the Talmud was the blueprint for Jewish self-government, the authoritative text consulted by the rabbis, who served as the community's judges. Jewish scholars of today who write about contemporary ethical issues — business ethics or biomedical ethics — invariably refer back to discussions in the Talmud and to the underlying legal and moral principles found there. The Talmud is taught in Jewish schools, although one has to be an advanced student to read and understand it in the original. And adult Jews still study the Talmud, either as individuals or in study circles, for edification and guidance, as well as for the pleasure of the intellectual challenge.

The Talmud has had such a wide-ranging influence on Jewish belief and practice from its own time down to the present, that we can truly say that one who knows only the Hebrew Scriptures does not know Judaism. There is admittedly much in the Talmud that is dated, much that reflects the prejudices and superstitions of a bygone age. But there is a great deal more within the Talmud that is of enduring value: its moral earnestness, its passion for righteousness and justice, its application of the tools of logic and intellect to religious life, its keen attentiveness to detail, and its insistence that personal holiness and a sense of God's presence can be found in the here and now through ethical living and the hallowing of everyday actions. To the rabbis of the Talmud, even the most mundane aspects of daily life have the potential of being transformed into a link with the Divine.

* * * * * *

The selections in this book were taken from Maurice H. Harris's **Hebraic Literature: Translations from the Talmud, Midrashim, and Kabbala**, New York and London, M. Walter

Dunne, 1901, part of the publisher's **Universal Classics Library.** The texts have been rearranged, so that they are grouped by topics, and I've made some slight changes in the translations. Since the vast bulk of the Talmud deals with Halacha and since the selections in Harris's book and in this small volume are drawn overwhelmingly from the Aggada, I've added my own translation of the first page of the Talmud, a passage dealing with the obligatory daily prayers, in order to convey some of the flavor of Talmudic reasoning and analysis. This selection is at the beginning of the section on Prayer.

A volume of this size is necessarily limited in scope. I conclude by offering some suggestions for further reading and study. Robert Goldenberg's chapter on the Talmud in Barry Holtz's **Back to the Sources: Reading the Classic Jewish Texts** (New York, Summit Books, 1984) and Adin Steinsaltz's **The Essential Talmud** (New York, Basic Books, 1976) are both excellent introductions to the methodology and contents of the Talmud. Jacob Neusner's **There We Sat Down: Talmudic Judaism in the Making** (Nashville, Abingdon, 1972) relates the history of how the Babylonian Talmud developed and how the values and teachings of the rabbis came to be accepted as authoritative. In **The Talmud**

for Beginners, Volume 1: Prayer
(Northvale, N.J., Jason Aronson,
1991), Judith Abrams presents and explains texts from the first tractate of the
Talmud, Berakhot. C. G. Montefiore
and H. Loewe's **A Rabbinic Anthology**
(New York, Schocken Books, 1974) is
the classic English-language anthology
of Aggada, culled not only from the
Talmud but also from the Midrashim.
The English translation of the Talmud
published by Soncino Press in London
has been in print for many years. Rabbi
Steinsaltz and his collaborators are cur-
rently issuing a new translation with
extensive commentaries, **The Talmud,
The Steinsaltz Edition**, published by
Random House. A number of volumes

have appeared, each containing one chapter of text with commentaries. The **Reference Guide** accompanying the Steinsaltz Talmud is a particularly valuable source of information about the Talmud and its historical background.

Barry A. Marks

Barry A. Marks, a graduate of Johns Hopkins University and the Jewish Theological Seminary, is rabbi of Temple Israel in Springfield, Illinois.

Torah

When Moses went up on high, the ministering angels asked, "What has one born of a woman to do among us?" "He has come to receive the Torah," was the Divine answer. "What!" they remonstrated again, "that cherished treasure which has lain with Thee for nine hundred and seventy-four generations before the world was created, art Thou about to bestow it upon flesh and blood? What is mortal man that Thou art mindful of him, and the son of earth that Thou takest account of him? O Lord! our

Lord! is not Thy name already suffi-
ciently exalted in the earth? Confer Thy
glory upon the heavens" (Ps. viii. 4, 5).
The Holy One — blessed be He! — then
called upon Moses to refute the objection
of the envious angels. "I fear," pleaded
he, "lest they consume me with the fiery
breath of their mouth." Thereupon, by
way of protection, he was bid approach
and lay hold of the throne of God; as it
is said (Job xxvi. 9), "He lays hold of
the face of His throne and spreads His
cloud over him." Thus encouraged,
Moses went over the Decalogue, and
demanded of the angels whether they
had suffered in Egyptian bondage and
dwelt among idolatrous nations, so as to
require the first commandment; or were

they so hardworked as to need a day of rest. Then the angels at once confessed that they were wrong in seeking to withhold the Torah from Israel, and they then repeated the words, "O Lord, how excellent is Thy name in all the earth!" (Ps. viii. 9), omitting the words, "Confer Thy glory upon the heavens." And not only so, but they positively befriended Moses, and each of them revealed to him some useful secret; as it is said (Ps. lxviii. 18), "Thou hast ascended on high, thou hast captured spoil, thou hast received gifts; because they have contemptuously called thee man."

Shabbat 88b

Once, the Roman Government issued a decree forbidding Israel to study the Torah. Whereupon Pappus, the son of Yehudah, one day found Rabbi Akiva teaching the Torah openly to multitudes, whom he had gathered round him to hear it. "Akiva," said he, "art thou not afraid of the Government?" "Listen," was the reply, "and I will tell thee how it is by way of a parable. Once, a fox, walking by a river's side, saw the fishes darting distractedly to and fro in the stream. The fox inquired of the fishes, 'From what, pray, are ye fleeing?' 'From the nets,' they replied, 'which the children of men have set to ensnare us.' 'Why, then,' rejoined the fox, 'not try the dry land with me, where you and I can live together, as our fathers managed to do before us?' 'Surely,' exclaimed they, 'thou art not he of whom we have heard so much as the most cunning of animals, for herein thou art not wise, but foolish. For if we have cause to fear where it is natural for us to live, how much more reason have we to do so where we would surely die!' Just so," continued Akiva, "is it with us who study the Torah, of which it is written (Deut. xxx, 20), 'It is thy life and the length of thy days;' for if we suffer while we study the Torah, how much more shall we if we neglect it?" Not many days after, it is related, this Rabbi Akiva was apprehended and thrown into prison. As it happened, they led him out for execution just at the time for reciting the prayer "Hear, O Israel, the Lord is our God, the Lord is one."

As the executioners tore his flesh with
currycombs, and as he was with long-
drawn breath sounding forth the word
"one," his soul departed from him.
Then came forth a voice from heaven
which said, "Blessed art thou, Rabbi
Akiva, for thy soul and the word "one"
left thy body together."

Berakhot 61b

Why are the words of the Torah
compared to fire? (Jer. xxiii. 29) Because, as fire does not burn when there
is but one piece of wood, so do the words
of the Torah not maintain the fire of life
when meditated on by one alone.

Ta'anit 7a

"Like the hammer that breaketh the rock in pieces" (Jer. xxiii. 29). As a hammer divideth fire into many sparks, so one verse of Scripture has many meanings and many explanations.

Sanhedrin 34a

By forty-eight things the Torah is acquired. These are study, attention, careful conversation, mental discernment, solicitude, reverential fear, meekness, geniality of soul, purity, attention to the wise, mutual discussion, debating, sedateness, learning in the Scripture and the Mishna, not dabbling in commerce, self-denial, moderation in sleep, aversion to gossip, etc., etc.

Avot 6:5

There was once a dispute between Rabbi Eliezer and the sages of the Mishna as to whether a baking-oven, constructed from certain materials and of a particular shape, was ritually clean or unclean. The former decided that it was clean, but the latter were of a contrary opinion. Having replied to all the objections the sages had brought against his decision, and finding that they still refused to acquiesce, the Rabbi turned to them and said, "If the Halacha (the law) is according to my decision, let this carob-tree attest." Whereupon the carob-tree uprooted itself and transplanted itself to a distance of one hundred, some say four hundred, yards from the spot. But the sages demurred and said, "We cannot admit the evidence of a carob-tree." "Well, then," said Rabbi Eliezer, "let this running brook be a proof;" and the brook at once reversed its natural course and flowed backwards. The sages refused to admit this proof also. "Then let the walls of the college bear witness that the law is according to my decision;" upon which the walls began to bend, and were about to fall, when Rabbi Joshua interposed and rebuked them, saying, "If the disciples of the sages wrangle with each other in the Halacha, what is that to you? Be ye quiet!" Therefore, out of respect to Rabbi Joshua, they did not fall, and out of respect to Rabbi Eliezer they did not resume their former upright position, but remained toppling, which they continue to do to this day. Then said Rabbi Eliezer to the sages, "Let Heaven itself testify that the Halacha is according to my judgment." And a Bath Kol or voice from heaven was heard, saying, "What have ye to do with Rabbi Eliezer? for the Halacha is on every point according to his decision!" Rabbi Joshua then stood up and proved from Scripture that even a voice from heaven was not to be regarded, "For Thou, O God, didst long ago write down in the Torah which Thou gavest on Sinai (Exod. xxiii. 2),[2] 'Thou shalt follow the multitude.'" We have it on the testimony of Elijah the prophet, given to Rabbi Nathan, on an oath, that with reference to this dispute about the oven God himself confessed and said, "My children have vanquished me! My children have vanquished me!"

Bava Metzia 59a

Rabbi Elazer ben Charsom inherited from his father a thousand towns and a thousand ships, and yet he went about with a leather sack of flour at his back, roaming from town to town and from province to province in order to study the Torah. This great Rabbi never once set eye on his immense patrimony, for he was engaged in the study of the Torah all day and all night long. And so strange was he to his own servants, that they, on one occasion, not knowing who he was, pressed him against his will to do a day's work as a menial; and though he pleaded

44

with them as a suppliant to be left alone
to pursue his studies in the Torah, they
refused, and swore, saying, "By the life
of Rabbi Elazer ben Charsom, our master, we will not let thee go till thy task
is completed." He then let himself be
enforced rather than make himself
known to them.

Yoma 35b

Rabbi Yossi ben Kisma relates, "I
once met a man in my travels and we
saluted one another. In reply to a question of his I said, 'I am from a great city
of sages and scribes.' Upon this he offered me a thousand thousand golden
denarii, and precious stones and pearls,
if I would agree to go and dwell in his
native place. But I replied, saying, 'If

thou were to give me all the gold and
silver, all the precious stones and pearls
in the world, I would not reside any-
where else than in a place where the
Torah is studied.' "

Avot 6:9

Rabbi Eliezer ben Hyrcanus was
twenty-two years of age when, contrary
to the wishes of his father, he went to
Rabban Yochanan ben Zakkai intending
to devote himself to the study of the
Torah. By the time he arrived at Rabban
Yochanan's he had been without food
four-and-twenty hours, and yet, though
repeatedly asked whether he had anything to eat, refused to confess he was
hungry. His father having come to know
where he was, went one day to the place

in order to disinherit him before the assembled Rabbis. It so happened that Rabban Yochanan was at that time lecturing before some of the great men of Jerusalem, and when he saw the father enter, he pressed Rabbi Eliezer to deliver an exposition. So startling and novel were his observations that Rabban Yochanan rose and styled him his own Rabbi, and thanked him in the name of the rest for the instruction he had afforded them. Then the father of Rabbi Eliezer said, "Rabbis, I came here for the purpose of disinheriting my son, but now I declare him sole heir of all that I have, to the exclusion of his brothers."

Avot d'Rabbi Nathan 6:3

God: Creation, Judgment and Providence

The five times the words "Bless the Lord, O my soul" (Ps. ciii. civ.), were repeated by David refer both to God and the soul. As God fills the whole world, so does the soul fill the whole body; as God sees and is not seen, so the soul sees and is not seen; as God nourishes the whole world, so does the soul nourish the whole body; as God is pure, so also is the soul pure; as God dwelleth in secret, so does the soul dwell in secret. Therefore let him who possesses these five properties praise Him to whom these five attributes belong.

Berakhot 10a

Certain philosophers once asked the elders at Rome, "If your God has no pleasure in idolatry, why does He not destroy the objects of it?" "And so He would," was the reply, "if only such objects were worshiped as the world does not stand in need of; but you idolaters will worship the sun and moon, the stars and the constellations. Should He destroy the world because of the fools there are in it? No! The world goes on as it has done all the same, but they who abuse it will have to answer for their

49

conduct. On your philosophy, when one steals a measure of wheat and sows it in his field it should by rights produce no crop; nevertheless the world goes on as if no wrong had been done, and they who abuse it will one day smart for it."

Avodah Zarah 54b

The greatness of God is infinite; for while with one die man impresses many coins and all are exactly alike, the King of kings, the Holy One — blessed be He! — with one die impresses the same image (of Adam) on all men, and yet not one of them is like his neighbor. So that every one ought to say, "For my sake is the world created."

Sanhedrin 4:5

Ten things were created during the twilight of the first Sabbath-eve. These were: — The well that followed Israel in the wilderness, the manna, the rainbow, the letters of the alphabet, the stylus, the tables of the law, the grave of Moses, the cave in which Moses and Elijah stood, the opening of the mouth of Balaam's ass, the opening of the earth to swallow the wicked (Korah and his clique). Rav Nechemiah said, in his father's name, also fire and the mule. Rav Yosheyah, in his father's name, added also the ram which Abraham offered up instead of Isaac, and the Shamir. Rav Yehudah says the tongs also, etc.

Pesachim 54a

To the ten things said to have been created on Sabbath-eve some add the rod of Aaron that budded and bloomed, and others add malignant demons and the garments of Adam.

Ibid.

Rav Yehuda said, in the name of Rav, ten things were created on the first day: — Heaven and earth, chaos and confusion, light and darkness, wind and water, the measure of day and the measure of night. "Heaven and earth," for it is written, "In the beginning God made the heavens and the earth." "Chaos and confusion," for it is written, "And the earth was chaos and confusion." "Light and darkness," for it is written, "And darkness was upon the face of the

abyss." "Wind and water," for it is
written, "The wind of God hovered over
the face of the waters." "The measure
of day and the measure of night," for it
is written, "Morning and evening were
one day."

Chagigah 12a

Rabbi Yochanan bar Chanena said:
— The day consists of twelve hours.
During the first hour Adam's dust was
collected from all parts of the world;
during the second it was made into a
lump; during the third his limbs were
formed; during the fourth his body was
animated; during the fifth he stood upon
his legs; during the sixth he gave names
to the animals; during the seventh he
associated with Eve; during the eighth

53

Cain and a twin sister were born; during the ninth Adam was ordered not to eat of the forbidden tree; during the tenth he fell, during the eleventh he was judged; and during the twelfth he was ejected from paradise; as it is said (Ps. xlix. 13), "Man (Adam) abode not one night in his dignity."

Sanhedrin 38b

There are twelve hours in the day: — The first three, the Holy One — blessed be He! — employs in studying the Torah; the next three He sits and judges the whole world; the third three He spends in feeding all the world; during the last three hours He sports with the leviathan; as it is said (Ps. civ. 26),

"This leviathan Thou hast created to play with it."

Avodah Zarah 3b

When the Holy One — blessed be He! — remembers that His children are in trouble among the nations of the world, He drops two tears into the great ocean, the noise of which startles the world from one end to the other, and causes the earth to quake.

Berakhot 59a

It is thus Rav Yoseph taught what is meant when it is written in Isaiah xii, 1, "I will praise Thee, O Lord, because Thou wast angry with me: Thine anger will depart and Thou wilt comfort me." "The text applies," he says, "to two men who were going abroad on a mercantile enterprise. One of them, having had a thorn run into his foot, had to forego his intended journey, and began in consequence to utter reproaches and blaspheme. Having afterward learned that the ship in which his companion had sailed had sunk to the bottom of the sea, he confessed his shortsightedness and praised God for His mercy."

Niddah 31a

Though ever since the destruction of the Temple the Sanhedrin has ceased to exist, the four kinds of capital punishment[3] have not failed to assert themselves. If a man incurs the penalty of death by stoning, he is in the course of Providence either punished by a fatal fall from a roof or slain by some beast of prey; if he has exposed himself to the penalty of death by burning, it happens that he is either burned to death in the end or mortally stung by a serpent; if the penalty of the law is that he should be beheaded for his offense, he meets his death either from the Government officer or by the hand of an assassin; if the penalty be strangulation, he is sure to be drowned or suffocated.

Sanhedrin 37b

Four times a year the world is subject to an ordeal of judgment: — At Passover, which is decisive of the fruits of the field; at Pentecost, which is decisive of the fruits of the garden; at the feast of Tabernacles, which is decisive in respect

of rain; on Near Year's Day, when all
who come into the world pass before the
Lord like sheep, as it is said (Ps. xxxiii.
15), "Who formed their hearts together;
who understandeth all their works."

Rosh Hashanah 16a

God is said to pray; for it is written
(Isa. 1vi.7), "Them will I bring to my
holy mountain, and make them joyful in
the house of my prayer." It is thus He
prays: "May it please me that my mercy
may overcome my anger, that all my
attributes may be invested with compassion, and that I may deal with my children in the attribute of kindness, and that
I judge them not by the strict letter of the
law."

Berakhot 7a

Ways
of
Righteousness

Once a Gentile came to Shammai,
and said, "Proselytize me, but on condition that thou teach me the whole
Torah, even the whole of it, while I stand
upon one leg." Shammai drove him off
with the builder's rod which he held in
his hand. When he came to Hillel with
the same challenge, Hillel converted him
by answering him on the spot, "That
which is hateful to thyself, do not do to

thy neighbor. This is the whole Torah, and the rest is its commentary."

Shabbat 31a

For the sake of one righteous man the whole world is preserved in existence, as it is written (Prov. x. 25), "The righteous man is an everlasting foundation."[4]

Yoma 38b

Simeon, the son of Gamliel, said, "I have been brought up all my life among the wise, and I have never found anything of more material benefit than silence.

Avot 1:17

Rabbi Akiva said, "Laughter and levity lead a man to lewdness; but tradition is a fence to the Torah, tithes are a fence to riches, vows are a fence to abstinence, while the fence of wisdom is silence."

Avot 3:13

He who slanders, he who receives slander, and he who bears false witness against his neighbor, deserve to be cast to the dogs.

Pesachim 118a

All animals will one day remonstrate with the serpent and say, "The lion treads upon his prey and devours it, the wolf tears and eats it, but thou, what profit hast thou in biting?'' The serpent will reply (Eccl. x,11), "I am no worse than a slanderer.''[5]

Ta'anit 8a

The third tongue (*i. e.*, slander) hurts three parties: the slanderer himself, the receiver of the slander, and the person slandered.

Arakhin 15b

If in time of national calamity a man withdraw himself from his kindred and refuse to share in their sorrow, his two guardian angels come and lay their hands upon his head and say, "This man has isolated himself from his country in the day of its need, let him not live to see and enjoy the day when God shall restore its prosperity." When the community is in trouble, let no man say, "I will go home and eat and drink, and say, Peace be unto thee, oh my soul!"; for to him Scripture hath solemnly said (Isa. xxii. 14), "Surely this iniquity shall not be purged from you till you die."

Ta'anit 11a

There are three crowns: — The crown of the Torah, the crown of the priesthood, and the crown of royalty; but the crown of a good name surpasses them all.

Avot 4:13

He who possesses these three virtues is a disciple of Abraham our father, and he who possesses the three contrary

vices is a son of Balaam the wicked. The
disciples of our father Abraham have a
kindly eye, a loyal spirit, and a lowly
mind. The disciples of Balaam the
wicked have an evil eye, a proud spirit,
and a grasping soul.

Avot 5:19

Over these three does God weep
every day: — Over him who is able to
study the Torah but neglects it; over him
who studies it amid difficulties hard to
overcome; and over the ruler who be-
haves arrogantly toward the community
he should protect.

Chagigah 5b

Six things bear interest in this world
and the capital remaineth in the world to

come: — Hospitality to strangers, visit-
ing the sick, devotion in prayer, early
attendance at the school of instruction,
the training of children to the study of
the Torah, and judging charitably of
one's neighbors.

Shabbat 127a

Choni, the Maagol,[6] once saw in his
travels an old man planting a carob-tree,
and he asked him when he thought the
tree would bear fruit. "After seventy
years," was the reply. "What!" said
Choni, "dost thou expect to live seventy
years and eat the fruit of thy labor?" "I
did not find the world desolate when I
entered it," said the old man: "and as
my fathers planted for me before I was

born, so I plant for those that will come after me."

Ta'anit 23a

Rav Hunna says, "A quarrel is like a breach in the bank of a river; when it is once made it grows wider and wider...." "A certain man used to go about and say, "Blessed is he who submits to a reproach and is silent, for a hundred evils depart from him." Shemuel said to Rav Yehuda, "It is written in Scripture (Prov. xvii. 14), 'The beginning of strife is as when one letteth out water.'" Strife is the beginning of a hundred lawsuits.

Sanhedrin 7a

Of two that quarrel, the one that first gives in shows the nobler nature.

Ketuvot 71b

A man once laid a wager with another that he would put Hillel out of temper. If he succeeded he was to receive, but if he failed he was to forfeit, four hundred zouzim. It was close upon Sabbath-eve, and Hillel was washing himself, when the man passed by his door, shouting, "Where is Hillel? where is Hillel?" Hillel wrapped his mantle around himself and went forth to see what the man wanted. "I want to ask thee a question," was the reply. "Ask on, my son," said Hillel. Whereupon the man said, "I want to know why the Babylonians have such round heads?" "A very important question, my son," said Hillel; "the reason is because their midwives are not clever." The man went away, but after an hour he returned, calling out as before, "Where is Hillel? where is Hillel?" Hillel again threw on his mantle and went out, meekly asking, "What now, my son?" "I want to know," said he, "why the people of Tadmor are weak-eyed?" Hillel replied, "This is an important question, my son, and the reason is this, they live in a sandy country." Away went the man, but in another hour's time he returned as before, crying out, "Where is Hillel? where is Hillel?" Out came Hillel again, as gentle as ever, blandly requesting to know what more he wanted. "I have a question to ask," said the man. "Ask on, my son," said Hillel. "Well, why have the Africans such broad feet?" said he. "Because they live in a marshy land," said Hillel. "I have many more questions to ask," said the man, "but I am afraid that I shall only try thy patience and make thee angry." Hillel, drawing his mantle around him, sat down and bade the man ask all the questions he wished. "Art thou Hillel," said he, "whom they call a prince in Israel?" "Yes," was the reply. "Well," said the other, "I pray there may not be many more in Israel like thee!" "Why," said Hillel, "how is that?" "Because," said the man, "I have betted four hundred zouzim that I could put thee out of temper, and I have lost them all through thee." "Be warned for the future," said Hillel; "better is it that thou shouldst lose four hundred zouzim, and four hundred more after them, than it should be said of Hillel he lost his temper!"

Shabbat 31a

Rav Ulla was once asked, "To what extent is one bound to honor his father and mother?" To which he replied, "See what a Gentile of Ashkelon once did, Dammah ben Nethina by name. The sages one day required goods to the value of sixty myriads, for which they were ready to pay the price, but the key of the store-room happened to be under the pillow of his father, who was fast asleep, and Dammah would not disturb him." Rabbi Eliezer was once asked the same question, and he gave the same answer, adding an interesting fact to the illustration: "The sages were seeking after precious stones for the high priest's breastplate, to the value of some sixty or eighty myriads of golden denarii, but the key of the jewel-chest happened to be under the pillow of his father, who was asleep at the time, and he would not wake him. In the following year, however, the Holy One — blessed be He! — rewarded him with the birth of a red heifer[7] among his herds, for which the sages readily paid him such a sum as compensated him fully for the loss he sustained in honoring his parent."

Kiddushin 31a

Charity and Deeds
of
Kindness

He who sets aside a portion of his wealth for the relief of the poor will be delivered from the judgment of Gehenna. This is illustsrated by the parable of the two sheep that attempted to ford a river; one was shorn of its wool and the other not; the former, therefore, managed to get over, but the latter, being heavy-laden, sank.

Gittin 7a

In three particulars is benevolence superior to almsgiving:[8] — Almsgiving is only the bestowment of money, but benevolence can be exercised by personal service as well. Alms can be given only to the poor, but benevolence can be shown no less to the rich. Alms are confined to the living, but benevolence may extend to both the dead and the living.

Sukkah 49b

It is related of Benjamin the righteous, who was keeper of the poor-box, that a woman came to him at a period of famine and solicited food. "By the worship of God," he replied, "there is nothing in the box." She then exclaimed, "O Rabbi, if thou dost not feed me I and my

seven children will starve." Upon which
he relieved her from his own private
purse. In course of time he fell ill and
was nigh unto death. Then the ministering angels interceded with the Holy One
— blessed be He! — and said, "Lord of
the Universe, Thou hast said he that
preserveth one single soul of Israel alive
is as if he had preserved the life of the
whole world; and shall Benjamin the
righteous, who preserved a poor woman
and her seven children, die so prema-
turely?" Instantly the death-warrant
which had gone forth was torn up, and
twenty-two years were added to his life.

Bava Batra 11a

Ten strong things were created in the
world (of which the one that comes after

is stronger than that which preceded). A mountain is strong, but iron can hew it in pieces; the fire weakens the iron; the water quenches the fire; the clouds carry off the water; the wind disperses the clouds; the living body resists the wind; fear enervates the body; wine abolishes fear; sleep overcomes wine, and death is stronger than all together; yet it is written (Prov. x. 2), "And righteousness delivereth from death."[9]

Bava Batra 10a

Turnus Rufus once said to Rabbi Akiva, "If your God is a friend to the poor, why doesn't he feed them?" To which he promptly replied, "That we by maintaining them may escape the condemnation of Gehenna." "On the contrary," said the Emperor, "the very fact of your maintaining the poor will condemn you to Gehenna. I will tell thee by a parable what this is like. It is as if a king of our own flesh and blood should imprison a servant who has offended him, and command that neither food nor drink should be given him, and as if one of his subjects in spite of him should go and supply him with both. When the king hears of it will he not be angry with that man? And ye are called servants, as it is said (Lev. xxv. 55), 'For unto me the children of Israel are servants.'" To this Rabbi Akiva replied, "And I too will tell thee a parable whereunto the thing is like. It is like a king of our own flesh and blood who, being angry with his son, imprisons him, and orders that neither food nor drink be given him, but one goes and gives him both to eat and drink. When the king hears of it will he not handsomely reward that man? And we are sons, as it is written (Deut. xiv,1), 'Ye are the sons of the Lord your God.'" "True," the Emperor replied, "ye are both sons and servants; sons when ye do the will of God; servants when ye do not; and now ye are not doing the will of God."

Bava Batra 10a

Once when Israel went up by pilgrimages to one of the three annual feasts in Jerusalem (see Exod. xxxiv. 23, 24), it so happened that there was no water to drink. Nicodemon ben Gorion therefore hired of a friendly neighbor twelve huge reservoirs of water promising to have them replenished by a given time, or failing this to forfeit twelve talents of silver. The appointed day came and still the drought continued, and therewith the scarcity of water; upon which the creditor appeared and demanded payment of the forfeit. Nicodemon answered, "There's time yet; the day is not over." The other chuckled to himself, inwardly remarking, "There's no chance now; there's been no rain all the season," and off he went to enjoy his bath. But Nicodemon sorrowful at his heart, wended his way to the Temple. After putting on his prayer scarf, he prayed, "Lord of the Universe! Thou knowest that I have not entered into this obligation for my own sake, but for Thy glory and for the benefit of Thy people."

While he prayed the clouds gathered overhead, the rain fell in torrents, and the reservoirs were filled to overflowing. On going out of the house of prayer he was met by the exacting creditor, who still urged that the money was due to him, as he said, the rain came after sunset. But in answer to prayer the clouds immediately dispersed, and the sun shone forth as brightly as ever.

Ta'anit 19b

A poor man once came to Rava and begged for a meal. "On what dost thou usually dine?" asked Rava. "On stuffed fowl and old wine," was the reply.

79

"What!" said Rava, "art thou not concerned about being so burdensome to the community?" He replied, "I eat nothing belonging to them, only what the Lord provides;" as we are taught (Ps. cxlv. 15), 'The eyes of all wait upon Thee, and Thou givest them their food in his season.' It is not said in *their* season, for so we learn that God provides for each individual in his season of need." While they were thus talking, in came Rava's sister, who had not been to see him for thirteen years, and she brought him as a present a stuffed fowl and some old wine also. Rava marveled at the coincidence, and turning to his poor visitor said, "I beg thy pardon, friend; rise, I pray thee, and eat."

Ketuvot 67b

80

Ulla and Rav Chasda were once traveling together, when they came up to the gate of the house of Rav Chena bar Chenelai. At the sight of it Rav Chasda stooped and sighed. "Why sighest thou?" asked Ulla, "seeing, as Rav says, sighing breaks the body in halves; for it is said (Ezek. xxi. 11), 'sigh, therefore, O son of man, with the breaking of thy loins;' and Rabbi Yochanan says a sigh breaks up the whole constitution; for it is said (Ezek. xxi. 12), 'And it shall be when they say unto thee, Wherefore sighest thou? that thou shalt answer, For the tidings because it cometh, and the whole heart shall melt,'" etc. To this Rav Chasda replied, "How can I help sighing over this house, where sixty

81

bakers used to be employed during the day, and sixty during the night, to make bread for the poor and needy; and Rav Chena had his hand always at his purse, for he thought the slightest hesitation might cause a poor but respectable man to blush; and besides he kept four doors open, one to each quarter of the heavens, so that all might enter and be satisfied? Over and above this, in time of famine he scattered wheat and barley abroad, so that they who were ashamed to gather by day might do so by night; but now this house has fallen into ruin, and ought I not to sigh?"

Berakhot 58b

Mar Ukva was in the habit of sending on the Day of Atonement four hundred zouzim to a poor neighbor of his. Once he sent the money by his own son, who returned bringing it back with him, remarking, "There is no need to bestow charity upon a man who, as I myself have seen, is able to indulge himself in expensive old wine." "Well," said his father, "since he is so dainty in his taste, he must have seen better days. I will therefore double the amount for the future." And this accordingly he at once remitted to him.

Ketuvot 67b

It is related of Rabbi Tarphon that he was very rich, but gave nothing to the poor. Once Rabbi Akiva met him and said, "Rabbi, dost thou wish me to purchase for thee a town or two?" "I do," said he, and at once gave him four thousand gold denarii. Rabbi Akiva took this sum and distributed it among the poor. Some time after Rabbi Tarphon met Rabbi Akiva and said, "Where are the towns thou purchasedst for me?" The latter seized hold of him by the arm and led him to the house of study, where, taking up a psalter, they read together till they came to this verse, "He hath dispersed, he hath given to the poor, his righteousness endureth forever" (Ps. cxii. 9). Here Rabbi Akiva paused and said, "This is the place I purchased for thee," and Rabbi Tarphon saluted him with a kiss.

Tract. Kallah.

Let thy house be open wide toward the south, the east, the west, and the north, just as Job, who made four entrances to his house, in order that the poor might find entrance without trouble from whatever quarter they might come.

Avot d'Rabbi Nathan 7:1

Justice

The same strict scrutiny is required in money matters as in cases of capital punishment; for it is said (Lev. xxiv. 22), "Ye shall have one manner of law." What distinction is there made between them? With regard to money matters three judges are deemed sufficient, while in cases of capital offense twenty-three are required.

Sanhedrin 4:1

Rabbi Yochanan said: — None were elected to sit in the High Council of the Sanhedrin except men of stature, of wis-

dom, of imposing appearance, and of
mature age; men who knew witchcraft
and seventy languages, in order that the
High Council of the Sanhedrin should
have no need of an interpreter.

Sanhedrin 17a

The Sanhedrin consisted of seventy-
one members. It is recorded that Rabbi
Yossi said, "Seldom was there conten-
tion in Israel, but the judicial court of
seventy-one sat in the Lishkath-hagaz-
ith, *i.e.*, Chamber of Hewn Stones in the
Temple. There were two ordinary courts
of justice consisting of twenty-three, one
of which sat at the entrance of the Temple-Mount, and the other at the entrance
of the ante-court; and also provincial
courts of justice, likewise comprising

twenty-three members, which held their sessions in all the cities of Israel. When an Israelite had a question to propose, he asked it first of the court in his own city. If they understood the case, they settled the matter; but if not, they applied to the court of the next city. If the neighboring justices could not decide, they went together and laid the case in debate before the court which held its session at the entrance of the Temple-Mount. If these courts, in turn, failed to solve the problem, they appealed to the court that sat in the entrance of the ante-court, where a discussion was entered into upon the moot points of the case; if no decision could be arrived at, they all referred to the supreme court of seventy-one, where the matter was finally decided by the majority of votes."

As the disciples of Shammai and Hillel multiplied who had not studied the law thoroughly, contentions increased in Israel to such an extent that the law lost its unity and became as two.

Sanhedrin 88b

The judge, says the Scripture, who for but one hour administers justice according to true equity, is a partner, as it were, with God in His work of creation.

Shabbat 10a

Despicable is the judge who judges for reward; yet his judgment is law, and must, as such, be respected.

Ketuvot 105a

A judge will establish the land if, like a king, he want nothing; but he will ruin it if, like a priest, he receive gifts from the threshing-floor.

Ketuvot 105b

Once when Shemuel was crossing a river in a ferryboat, a man lent a sustaining hand to prevent him from falling. "What," said the Rabbi, "have I done for thee, that thou art so attentive with thy services?" The man replied, "I have a lawsuit before thee." "In that case," said Shemuel, "thy attention has disqualified me from judging in thy lawsuit."

Ameimar was once sitting in judgment, when a man stepped forward and removed some feathers that were clinging to his hair. Upon this the judge asked, "What service have I done thee?" The man replied, "I have a case to bring up before thee, my lord." The Rabbi replied, "Thou hast disqualified me from being judge in the matter."

Mar Ukva once noticed a man politely step up and cover some saliva which lay on the ground before him. "What have I done for thee?" said the Rabbi. "I have a case to bring before thee," said the man. "Thou hast bribed me with thy kind attention," said the Rabbi; "I cannot be thy judge."

Rabbi Ishmael, son of Rabbi Yossi, had a gardener who regularly brought him a basket of grapes every Friday. One time when the gardener brought it on a Thursday, the Rabbi asked him the reason why he had come a day earlier. "My lord," said the gardener, "because I have a lawsuit before thee to-day, I thought by so doing I might save myself the journey to-morrow." Upon hearing this the Rabbi both refused to take the basket of grapes, though they were really his own, and declined to act as judge in the process. He, however, appointed two Rabbis to judge the case in his stead, and while they were investigating the evidence in the litigation he kept pacing up and down, and saying to himself, if the gardener were sharp he might say so-and-so in his own behalf. He was at one time on the point of speaking in defense of his gardener, when he checked himself and said, "The receivers of bribes may well look to their souls. If I who have not even taken a bribe of what was my own feel partial, how perverted must the disposition become of those who receive bribes at the hands of others!"

Ketuvot 105a

Let judges know with Whom and before Whom they judge, and Who it is that will one day exact account of their judgments; for it is said (Ps. lxxxii,1), "God standeth in the assembly of God, and judgeth with the judges."

Sanhedrin 6b

A judge who does not judge justly causeth the Shechinah to depart from

Israel; for it is said (Ps. xii. 6), "For the oppression of the poor, the sighing of the needy, now will I depart, saith the Lord."

Sanhedrin 7a

Sin and
Repentance

"He caused the lame to mount on the
back of the blind, and judged them both
as one." Antoninus said to Rabbi, [10]
"Body and soul might each plead right
of acquittal at the day of judgment."
"How so?" he asked. "The body might
plead that it was the soul that had sinned,
and urge, saying, 'See, since the depar-
ture of the soul I have lain in the grave
as still as a stone.' And the soul might
plead, 'It was the body that sinned, for
since the day I left it, I have flitted about

in the air as innocent as a bird.'" To which Rabbi replied and said, "Whereunto this thing is like, I will tell thee in a parable. It is like unto a king who had an orchard with some fine young fig trees planted in it. He set two gardeners to take care of them, of whom one was lame and the other blind. One day the lame one said to the blind, 'I see some fine figs in the garden; come, take me on thy shoulders, and we will pluck them and eat them.' By and by the lord of the garden came, and missing the fruit from the fig trees, began to make inquiry after them. The lame one, to excuse himself, pleaded, 'I have no legs to walk with;' and the blind one, to excuse himself, pleaded, 'I have no eyes to see with.'

What did the lord of the garden do? He caused the lame to mount upon the back of the blind, and judged them both as one." So likewise will God re-unite soul and body, and judge them both as one together; as it is written (Ps. 1. 4), "He shall call to the heavens from above, and to the earth, that He may judge His people." "He shall call to the heavens from above," that alludes to the soul; "and to the earth, that He may judge His people," that refers to the body.

Sanhedrin 91 a,b

Rabbi Yochanan and Rabbi Yonathan traveled one day together; they came to two roads, one of which led by the door of a place devoted to the worship of idols, and the other by a place of ill fame. Upon which one said to the other, "Let us go by the former, because our inclination to the evil that waylays us there is already extinguished." "Nay, rather," said the other, "let us go by the latter, and curb our desires; so shall we receive a reward in recompense." In this resolution they went on, and as they passed the place the women humbled themselves before them and withdrew ashamed into their chambers. Then Yochanan asked the other, "How didst thou know that this would occur to us?" He made answer, "From what is written (in Prov. ii, 11), 'Discretion (in the law) shall preserve thee.'"

Avodah Zarah 17a,b

The Rabbis teach concerning the two kidneys in man, that one counsels him to do good and the other to do evil; and it appears that the former is situated on the right side and the latter on the left. Hence it is written (Eccl. x. 2), "A wise man's heart is at his right hand, but a fool's heart is at his left."

Berakhot 61a

The first step in transgression is evil thought, the second scoffing, the third pride, the fourth outrage, the fifth idleness, the sixth hatred, and the seventh an evil eye.

Derech Eretz Zuta, chap. 6.

Rabbi Meir saith, "Great is repentance, because for the sake of one that truly repenteth the whole world is pardoned; as it is written (Hosea xiv. 5), 'I will heal their backsliding, I will love them freely, for mine anger is turned away from him.'" It is not said, "from them," but "from him."

Yoma 86b

"Repent one day before thy death." In reference to which Rabbi Eliezer was asked by his disciples, "How is a man to repent one day before his death, since he does not know on what day he shall die?" "So much the more reason is there," he replied, "that he should repent to-day, lest he die to-morrow; and repent to-morrow, lest he die the day after: and thus will all his days be penitential ones."

Avot d'Rabbi Nathan 15:4

Four things cancel the decrees of Heaven: — Alms, prayer, change of name, and reformation of conduct. Alms, as it is written (Prov. x. 2), "But alms (more correctly, righteousness) delivereth from death." Prayer as it is written (Ps. cvii. 6), "Then they cried unto the Lord in their trouble, and He delivered them out of their distresses." Change of name, as it is said (Gen. xvii. 15, 16), "As for Sarai thy wife, thou shalt not call her name Sarai, but Sarah shall be her name." And after this change of name it is written, "And I will bless her, and give thee a son of her." Reformation of conduct, as it is written (Jonah iii. 10), "And God saw their works," and "God repented of the evil," etc. Some say also change of residence

has the effect of turning back the decree
of Heaven (Gen. xii,1), "And the Lord
said unto Abram, Get thee out of thy
country;" and then it is said, "I will
make of thee a great nation."

Rosh Hashanah 16b

A man may obtain forgiveness after
the third transgression, but if he repeat
the offense a fourth time, he is not
pardoned again; for it is said (Amos ii.
4), "For three transgressions of Judah,
and for four, I will not turn away the
punishment thereof;" and again (Job
xxxiii. 29), "Lo! all these things doth
God two or three times" (and so infer-
entially not four times) "with man to
bring back his soul from the pit."

Yoma 86b

Temple
and
Priesthood

The number of high priests who officiated in succession during the 410 years of the first Temple[11] was only eighteen, but the number who held office during the 420 years of the second Temple amounted to more than three hundred, most of them having died within a year after their entrance upon the office. The reason assigned by the Talmud for the long lives of the former and short lives of the latter is the text given in

Prov. x. 27, "The fear of the Lord prolongeth days, but the years of the wicked shall be shortened."

Yoma 9a

Before a priest could be admitted into active service in the Temple he had to undergo bodily inspection at the hands of the syndicate of the Sanhedrin. If they found the least defect in his body, even a mole with hair upon it, he was ordered to dress in black and be dismissed; but if he was perfectly free from blemish, he was arrayed in white, and at once introduced to his brother priests and official duties.

Yoma 19a

So long as there is a diadem on the head of the priest, there is a crown on the head of every man. Remove the diadem from the head of the high priest and you take away the crown from the head of all the people. (See Ezek. xxi, 31)

Gittin 7a

Ten facts witness to the presence of a supernatural power in the Temple: — No premature birth was ever caused by the odor of the sacrifices; the carcasses never became putrid; no fly was ever to be seen in the slaughter-houses; the high-priest was never defiled on the Day of Atonement; no defect was ever found in the wave-sheaf,[12] the two wave-loaves, or the shewbread; however closely crowded the people were, every one had room enough for prostration; no serpent or scorpion ever stung a person in Jerusalem; and no one had ever to pass the night without sleeping-accommodation in the city.

Yoma 21a

There were thirteen horn-shaped collecting-boxes, and thirteen tables, and thirteen devotional bowings in the Temple service. Those who belonged to the houses of Rabban Gamliel and of Rabbi Chananiah, the president of the priests, bowed fourteen times. This extra act of bowing was directed to the quarter of the wood store, in consequence of a tradition they inherited from their ancestors that the Ark of the Covenant was hidden in that locality. The origin of the tradition was this: — A priest, being once engaged near the wood store, and observing that part of the plaster differed from the rest, went to tell his companions, but died before he had time to relate his discovery. Thus it became known for certain that the Ark was hidden there.

Shekalim 6:1,2

Rabban Simeon ben Gamliel, in the name of Rabbi Joshua, says, "Since the destruction of the Temple a day has not passed without a curse; the dew does not come down with a blessing, and the fruits have lost their proper taste." Rabbi Yossi adds, "Also the lusciousness of the fruit is gone." Rabbi

Shimon ben Elazar says, "With the cessation of the laws of ritual purity, the taste and aroma (of the fruit) has disappeared, and with the cessation of tithes, the richness of the corn." The sages say, "Lewdness and witchcraft ruin everything."

Sotah 9:12,13

There was a place for collecting the ashes in the middle of the altar, and there were at times in it nearly as much as three hundred cors (equal to about 2830 bushels) of ashes. On Rava remarking that this must be an exaggeration, Rav Ammi said the law, the prophets, and the sages are wont to use hyperbolic language. Thus the law speaks of "Cities great and walled up to heaven" (Deut.

i. 28); the prophets speak of "the earth rent with the sound of them" (I Kings i. 40); the sages speak as above and also as follows. There was a golden vine at the entrance of the Temple, trailing on crystals, on which devotees who could used to suspend offerings of fruit and grape clusters. "It happened once," said Rabbi Elazer ben Rabbi Zadok, "that three hundred priests were counted off to clear the vine of the offerings."

Chullin 90b

Prayer
and
Thanksgiving

From what time do we recite the
Shema in the evening? From the time
when the priests (who have been ritually
unclean and have immersed themselves)
enter to eat their heave-offering until the
end of the first watch — these are the
words of Rabbi Eliezer. But the Sages
say: until midnight. Rabban Gamliel
says: until dawn. Once Rabban Gamliel's sons returned late from a feast and
told him, "we have not yet recited the

Shema." He said to them, "If dawn has not yet arrived, you are still obligated to recite it." Moreover, any place the Sages say "until midnight," the commandment may be fulfilled until dawn. The burning of fat and limbs of the sacrificial animals on the altar may go on until dawn. In regard to all sacrificial offerings which must be consumed within a day, the commandment may be fulfilled until dawn. If so, why did the Sages say "until midnight"? In order to keep people far from transgression.[13]

On what does the authority here base himself, when he begins by inquiring when we may recite the evening Shema? Where do we learn of an obligation to recite the Shema? Moreover, why does he speak of the evening Shema first? Let him teach first about the morning Shema. He is basing himself on Scripture (Deut. vi.7), "thou shalt speak of them, when thou liest down and when thou risest up." And thus he teaches: When is the time for reciting the Shema of "lying down"? From the time when the priests enter to eat their heave-offering. Alternately, you might say, he is following the order in which the world was created, as it is written (Gen. i,5), "there was evening, and there was morning". If so, why later on in this chapter of the Mishna does the text say: In the morning one recites two benedictions before the Shema and two afterward, and in the evening one recites two benedictions before and two afterward? There too, let him teach about the evening first. The Mishna begins by speaking of the evening Shema, then proceeds to teach about the morning Shema. Then, since the text is dealing with matters pertaining to the morning, it goes on to explain them (how many benedictions are recited before and after the Shema) before going back to explain matters pertaining to the evening.

The Mishna says that the Shema is recited from the time the priests enter to eat of their heave-offering. When is that? From the time the stars appear in the sky. Why then doesn't the Mishna teach us directly that the Shema is recited from the time the stars appear in the sky?

The text, though dealing with the question of reciting the Shema, is intended to teach us something else indirectly, namely that priests who have been unclean and have immersed themselves may eat of the heave-offering when the stars appear in the sky. This teaches us that the failure to offer a sacrifice of expiation does not prevent the priest from eating the heave-offering, as it is written (Lev. xxii,7), "and when the sun sets, he shall be clean." Thus, the priest is prevented from eating the heave-offering until the sun sets, but the failure to offer a sacrifice of expiation doesn't prevent him from eating it.

Berakhot 2a

"Hear O Israel, the Lord our God is one Lord!" (Deut. vi. 4.) Whosoever prolongs the utterance of the word *one*, shall have his days and years prolonged to him.

Berakhot 13b

He who three times a day repeats David's psalm of praise (Ps. cxlv.) may be sure of an inheritance in the world to come.

Berakhot 4b

Four are in duty bound to return thanks to God: — They that have returned from a voyage at sea (Ps. cvii. 23, 24, 31); those who have traveled in the desert (verses 4-8); they who have recovered from a serious illness (verses

17-21); and those that are liberated from prison (verses 10-15).

Berakhot 54b

Where is it taught that when ten join together in prayer the Shechinah is with them? In Ps. lxxxii,1,[14] where it is said, "God standeth in the congregation of the mighty."

Berakhot 6a

A certain disciple prayed before Rabbi Chanina, and said, "O God! who art great, mighty, formidable, magnificent, strong, terrible, valiant, powerful, real and honored!" He waited until he had finished, and then said to him, "Hast thou ended all the praises of thy God? Need we enumerate so many? As for us, even the three terms of praise which we usually repeat, "great, mighty, exalted" we should not dare to utter had not Moses, our master, pronounced them in the Torah (Deut. x. 17), and had not the men of the Great Synagogue ordained them for prayer; and yet thou hast repeated so many and still seemest inclined to go on. It is as if one were to compliment a king because of his silver, who is master of a thousand thousands of gold denarii. Wouldst thou think that becoming?"

Berakhot 33b

Sabbath
and
Holidays

When Rabbi Shimon ben Yochai and
his son, Rabbi Elazar, came out of their
cave on a Friday afternoon,[15] they saw
an old man hurrying along with two
bunches of myrtle in his hand. "What,"
said they, accosting him, "dost thou
want with these?" "To smell them in
honor of the Sabbath," was the reply.
"Would not one bunch," they remarked,
"be enough for that purpose" "Nay,"
the old man replied; "one is in honor of

'Remember'' (Exod. xx,8); and one in honor of 'Keep' (Deut. v. 12).''[16] Thereupon Rabbi Shimon remarked to his son, "Behold how the commandments are regarded by Israel!"

Shabbat 33b

When a man is dangerously ill, the law grants dispensation, for it says, "You may break one Sabbath on his behalf, that he may be preserved to keep many Sabbaths."

Shabbat 151b

"Every man as he goes on the eve of the Sabbath from the synagogue to his house is escorted by two angels, one of which is a good angel and the other an evil. When the man comes home and finds the lamps lit, the table spread, and the bed in order, the good angel says, "May the coming Sabbath be even as the present;" to which the evil angel (though with reluctance) is obliged to say, "Amen." But if all be in disorder, then the bad angel says, "May the coming Sabbath be even as the present," and the good angel is (with equal reluctance) obliged to say "Amen" to it.

Shabbat 119b

If Israel kept only two Sabbaths, according to the strict requirement of the law, they would be freed at once from their exile; for it is written (Isa. lvi. 4, 7), "Thus saith the Lord unto the eunuchs that keep my Sabbaths, Even them will I bring to my holy mountain."

Shabbat 118b

Six blasts of the horn were blown on Sabbath-eve. The first was to set free the laborers in the fields from their work; those that worked near the city waited for those that worked at a distance and all entered the place together. The second blast was to warn the citizens to suspend their employments and shut up their shops. At the third blast the women were to have ready the various dishes they had prepared for the Sabbath and to light the lamps in honor of the day. Then three more blasts were blown in succession, and the Sabbath commenced.

Shabbat 35b

There was once a man named Joseph, who was renowned for honoring the Sabbath-day. He had a rich neighbor, a Gentile, whose property a certain fortune-teller had said would eventually revert to Joseph the Sabbatarian. To frustrate this prediction the Gentile disposed of his property, and with the proceeds of the sale he purchased a rare and costly jewel which he fixed to his turban. On crossing a bridge a gust of wind blew his turban into the river and a fish swallowed it. This fish being caught, was brought on a Friday to market, and, as luck would have it, it was bought by Joseph in honor of the coming Sabbath. When the fish was cut up the jewel was found, and this Joseph sold it for thirteen purses of gold denarii. When his neighbor met him, he acknowledged that he who despised the Sabbath the Lord of the Sabbath would be sure to punish.

Shabbat 119a

They associated with the high priest the senior elders of the Sanhedrin, who read over to him the agenda of the day, and then said to him, "My lord high priest, read thou for thyself; perhaps thou hast forgotten it, or maybe thou hast not learned it at all."[17] On the day before the Day of Atonement he was taken to the East Gate where they caused oxen, rams, and lambs to pass before him, that he might become well-versed and expert in his official duties. During the whole of the seven (preparatory) days neither victuals nor drink were withheld from him, but toward dusk on the eve of the Day of Atonement they did not allow him to eat much, for much food induces sleep. Then the elders of the Sanhedrin surrendered him to the elders of the priesthood, and these conducted him to the hall of the house of Abtinas, and there they swore him in; and after bidding him good-bye, they went away. In administering the oath they said, "My lord high priest, we are ambassadors of the Sanhedrin; thou art our ambassador and the ambassador of the Sanhedrin as well. We adjure thee, by Him who causes His name to dwell in this house, that thou alter not anything that we have told thee!" Then they parted, both they and he weeping. He wept because they suspected he was a Sadducee, and they wept because the penalty for wrongly suspecting persons is scourging. If he was a learned man he preached (during the night); if not, learned men preached before him. If he was a ready reader, he read; if not, others read to him. What were the books that were read to him? Job, Ezra, and the Chronicles. Zechariah the son of Kevootal says, "I have often read before him the Book of Daniel." If he became drowsy, the juniors of the priestly order snapped their middle fingers before him, and said, "My lord high priest, stand up and cool thy feet upon the pavement." Thus they

kept him engaged till the time of slaugh-
tering (the sacrifices).

Yoma 18 a,b,; 19b

The Rabbis teach that the precept
relating to the lighting of a candle at the
Feast of Chanuka applies to a whole
household, but that those who are particular light a candle for each individual
member, and those that are extremely
particular light eight candles on the first
day, seven on the second, decreasing the
number by one each day. This is according to the school of Shammai; but the
school of Hillel says that he should light
one on the first day, two on the second,
increasing the number by one each of the
eight days of the festival.... What is the

origin of the feast of Chanuka? On the twenty-fifth day of Kislev (about December), the eight days of Chanuka commence, during which time no funeral oration is to be made, nor public fast to be decreed. When the Gentiles (Greeks) entered the second Temple, it was thought they had defiled all the holy oil they found in it; but when the Hasmoneans prevailed and conquered them, they sought and found still one jar of oil stamped with the seal of the High Priest, and therefore undefiled. Though the oil it contained would only have sufficed for one day, a miracle was performed, so that the oil lasted to the end of the week (during which time more oil was provided and consecrated for the future

service of the Temple). On the anniver-
sary of this occasion the Feast of
Chanuka was instituted.[18]

Shabbat 21b

No food may be eaten on Passover-
eve from the time of the offering of the
evening sacrifice (in order that abstinence may whet the appetite for the
matzot). Even the poorest in Israel may
not break his fast till the hour of reclin-
ing; nor is he to partake of less than four
glasses of wine, even though he has been
reduced so low as to subsist on the
porridge doled out by public charity.

Pesachim 99b

On the ninth day of Av[19] one must
abstain from eating and drinking, and

anointing one's self, and wearing shoes, and marital intercourse. He may not read the Bible, the Talmud, the Midrash, the Halachot, or the Haggadot, excepting such portions as he is not in the habit of reading, such he may then read. The Lamentations, Job, and the hard works of Jeremiah should engage his study. Children should not go to school on this day, because it is said (Ps. xix. 8), "The statutes of the Lord are right, rejoicing the heart."

Ta'anit 30a

He who does any work on the ninth of Av will never see even a sign of blessing. The sages say, whoso does any work on that day and does not lament over Jerusalem will never see her joy;

for it is said (Isa. lxvi. 10), "Rejoice ye with Jerusalem, and be glad with her; rejoice for joy, all ye that mourn for her."

Ta'anit 30b

Israel: Covenant
and
Election

"Thou hast acknowledged the Lord
this day to be thy God; and the Lord hath
acknowledged thee this day to be His
peculiar people" (Deut. xxvi. 17, 18).
The Holy One — blessed be He! — said
unto Israel, "Ye have made Me a name
in the world, as it is written (Deut. vi.
4), 'Hear, O Israel, the Lord our God is
one Lord;' and so I will make you a
name in that world, as it is said (I Chron.

xvii. 21), 'And what one nation in the earth is like Thy people Israel?'"

Chagigah 3a

"Zion said, The Lord hath forsaken and forgotten me" (Isa. xlix. 14). The community of Israel once pleaded thus with the Holy One — blessed be He! — "Even a man who marries a second wife still bears in mind the services of the first, but Thou, Lord, hast forgotten me." The Holy One — blessed be He! — replied, "Daughter, I have created twelve constellations in the firmament, and for each constellation I have created thirty armies, and for each army thirty legions, each legion containing thirty divisions, each division thirty cohorts, each cohort having thirty camps, and in each camp hang suspended 365,000 myriads of stars, as many thousands of myriads as there are days in the year; all these have I created for thy sake, and yet thou sayest, 'Thou hast forsaken and forgotten me!' Can a woman forget her sucking-child, that she should not have compassion on the son of her womb? Yea, they may forget, yet will I not forget thee.''

Berakhot 32b

Rabban Gamliel, Rabbi Eliezer ben Azaryah, Rabbi Joshua, and Rabbi Akiva once went on a journey to Rome, and at Puteoli they already heard the noisy din of the city, though at a distance of a hundred and twenty miles. At the sound all shed tears except Akiva, who

began to laugh. "Why laughest thou?"
they asked. "Why do you cry?" he
retorted. They answered, "These Romans, who worship idols of wood and
stone and offer incense to stars and
planets, abide in peace and quietness,
while our Temple, which was the foot-
stool of our God, is consumed by fire;
how can we help weeping?" "That is
just the very reason," said he, "why I
rejoice; for if such be the lot of those
who transgress His laws, what shall the
lot of those be who observe and do
them?"

Makkot 24b

At the time when Israel in their
eagerness first said, "We will do," and
then, "We will hear" (Exod. xxiv, 7),[20]

there came sixty myriads of ministering angels to crown each Israelite with two crowns, one for "we will do" and one for "we will hear." But when after this Israel sinned, there came down a hundred and twenty myriads of destroying angels and took the crowns away from them, as it is said (Exod. xxxiii. 6), "And the children of Israel stripped themselves of their ornaments by Mount Horeb." Resh Lakish says, "The Holy One — blessed be He! — will, in the future, return them to us; for it is said (Isa. xxxv. 10), 'The ransomed of the Lord shall return and come to Zion with songs and everlasting joy upon their heads,' *i.e.*, the joy they had in days of yore."

Shabbat 88a

135

Persecution
and
Martyrdom

Once a Jewish mother with her seven sons suffered martyrdom at the hands of the Emperor. The sons, when ordered by the latter to do homage to the idols of the Empire, declined, and justified their disobedience by quoting each a simple text from the sacred Scriptures. When the seventh was brought forth, it is related that Cæsar, for appearance' sake, offered to spare him if only he would stoop and pick up a ring from the ground which had been dropped on purpose. "Alas for thee, O Cæsar!" answered the boy; "if thou art so zealous for thine honor, how much more zealous ought we to be for the honor of the Holy One — blessed be He!" On his being led away to the place of execution, the mother craved and obtained leave to give him a farewell kiss. "Go, my child," said she, "and say to Abraham, Thou didst build an altar for the sacrifice of one son, but I have erected altars for seven sons." She then turned away and threw herself down headlong from the roof and expired, when the echo of a voice was heard exclaiming (Ps. cxiii. 9), "The joyful mother of children."

Gittin 57b

Cæsar once said to Rabbi Tanchum, "Come, now, let us be one people." "Very well," said Rabbi Tanchum, "only we, being circumcised cannot possibly become like you; if, however, ye become circumcised we shall be alike in that regard anyhow, and so be as one people." The Emperor said, "Thou hast reasonably answered, but the Roman law is, that he who prevails over the ruler in argument and puts him to silence shall be cast to the lions." The word was no sooner uttered than the Rabbi was thrown into the den, but the lions stood aloof and did not even touch him. A Sadducee, who looked on, remarked, "The lions do not devour him because they are not hungry," but, when at the

138

royal command, the Sadducee himself
was thrown in, he had scarcely reached
the lions before they fell upon him and
began to tear his flesh and devour him.

Sanhedrin 39a

Four hundred boys and as many girls
were once kidnapped and torn from their
relations. When they learned the purpose of their capture, they all exclaimed,
"Better drown ourselves in the sea; then
shall we have an inheritance in the world
to come." The eldest then explained to
them the text (Ps. lxviii. 23), "The Lord
said, I will bring again from Bashan; I
will bring again from the depths of the
sea." "From Bashan," *i.e.*, from the
teeth of the lion;[21] "from the depths of
the sea," *i.e.*, those that drown them-

selves in the sea. When the girls heard this explanation they at once jumped all together into the sea, and the boys with alacrity followed their example. It is with reference to these that Scripture says (Ps. xliv. 23), "For thy sake we are killed all the day long; we are counted as sheep for the slaughter."

Gittin 57b

Health and Diet

It were better to cut the hands off than to touch the eye, or the nose, or the mouth, or the ear, etc., with them without having first washed them. Unwashed hands may cause blindness, deafness, foulness of breath, or a polypus. It is taught that Rabbi Nathan has said, "The evil spirit Bath Chorin, which rests upon the hands at night, is very strict; he will not depart till water is poured upon the hands three times over."

Shabbat 109a

Three effects are ascribed to Babylonian broth (which was made of moldy bread, sour milk, and salt): — It retards the action of the heart, it affects the eyesight, and emaciates the body.

Pesachim 42a

Dates are good after meals in the morning and in the evening, but hurtful in the afternoon; on the other hand, at noon they are most excellent, and an antidote to these three maladies: — Evil thought, constipation, and hemorrhoids.

Ketuvot 10b

Beware of these three things: — Do not sit too much, for it brings on hemorrhoids; do not stand too much, for it is bad for the heart; do not walk too much, for it is hurtful to the eyes. But sit a third, stand a third, and walk a third.

Ketuvot 111a

One cup of wine is good for a woman, two are disgraceful, three demoralizing, and four brutalizing.

Ketuvot 65a

If one does not walk, say four cubits, before falling asleep after a meal, that which he has eaten, being undigestible, causes foulness of breath.

Shabbat 41a

These things are said concerning garlic: — It nourishes, it glows inwardly, it brightens the complexion, and increases virility. Some say that it is a philtre for love, and that it exterminates jealousy.

Bava Kama 82a

The Rabbis have taught thirteen things respecting breakfast (morning-morsel): — It counteracts the effects of heat, cold or draught; it protects from malignant demons; it makes wise the simple by keeping the mind in a healthy condition; it enables a man to come off clear from a judicial inquiry; it qualifies him both to learn and to teach the law; it makes him eagerly listened to, to have a retentive memory, etc.

Bava Metzia 107b

Rav Mari reports that Rabbi Yochanan had said, "He who indulges in the practice of eating lentils once in thirty days keeps away quinsy, but they are not good to be eaten regularly because by them the breath is corrupted.'' He used also to say that mustard eaten once in thirty days drives away sickness, but if taken every day the action of the heart is apt to be affected.

Berakhot 40a

Marriage

The Jew that has no wife is not a man; for it is written (Gen. v. 2), "Male and female created He them and called their name man." To which Rabbi Eleazar adds, "So every one who has no landed property is no man; for it is written (Ps. cxv. 16), 'The heaven, even the heavens, are the Lord's, but the earth (the land, that is), hath He given to the children of man.'"

Yevamot 63a

He who does not cheer the bride-groom whose wedding feast he has en-

joyed transgresses against the five voices
(mentioned in Jer. xxxiii, 11): — "The
voice of joy, the voice of gladness, the
voice of the bridegroom, and the voice
of the bride, the voice of them that shall
say 'Praise ye the Lord of Hosts.'"

Berakhot 6b

Rabban Simeon ben Gamliel has said
there were no such gala-days for Israel
as the fifteenth of Av and the Day of
Atonement, when the young maidens of
Jerusalem used to resort to the vineyard
all robed in white garments, that were
required to be borrowed, lest those
should feel humiliated who had none of
their own. There they danced gleefully,
calling to the lookers-on and saying,
"Young men, have a care; the choice

147

you now make may have conse-
quences."

Ta'anit 16b

If a man remain unmarried after the
age of twenty, his life is a constant
transgression. The Holy One — blessed
be He! — waits until that period to see
if one enters the matrimonial state, and
curses his bones if he remain single.

Kiddushin 29b

Death
and
Mourning

Rabbi the Holy,[22] when dying, lifted up his ten fingers toward heaven and said: — "Lord of the universe, it is open and well-known unto Thee that with these ten fingers I have labored without ceasing in the Torah, and never sought after any worldly profit with even so much as my little finger; may it therefore please Thee that there may be peace in my rest!" A voice from heaven immediately responded (Isa. lvii. 2), "He shall enter peace: they shall rest in their beds."

Ketuvot 104b

"There are two ways before me, one leading into Paradise, the other into Gehenna." When Yochanan, the son of Zakkai, was sick unto death, his disciples came to visit him; and when he saw them he wept, upon which his disciples exclaimed, "Light of Israel! Pillar of the right! Mighty Hammer! why weepest thou?" He replied, "If I were going to be led into the presence of a king, who is but flesh and blood to-day here and to-morrow in the grave, whose anger with me could not last forever, whose sentence against me, were it even unto death, could not endure forever, and

150

whom perhaps I might pacify with words or bribe with money, yet for all that should I weep; but now that I am about to enter the presence of the King of kings, the Holy One — blessed be He forever and ever! — Whose anger would be everlasting, Whose sentence of death or imprisonment admits of no reprieve, and Who is not to be pacified with words nor bribed with money, and in Whose presence there are two roads before me, one leading into Paradise and the other into Gehenna, should I not weep?" Then they entreated him, "Rabbi, give us thy farewell blessing;" and he said unto them, "Oh that the fear of God may be as much upon you as the fear of man."

Berakhot 28b

151

If we meet a friend during any of the thirty days of his mourning for a deceased relative, we must condole with him but not salute him; but after that time he may be saluted but not condoled with. If a man (because he has no family) re-marries within thirty days of the death of his wife, he should not be condoled with at home (lest it might hurt the feelings of his new partner); but if met with out of doors, he should be addressed in an undertone of voice, accompanied with a slight inclination of the head.

Mo'ed Katan 21b

During the thirty days of mourning for deceased friends or relatives, the

bereaved should not trim their hair; but
if they have lost their parents, they are
not to attend to such matters until their
friends force them to do so.

Mo'ed Katan 22b

If a man has lost a relative, he is
forbidden to engage in business until
thirty days after the death. In the case of
the death of a father or a mother, he is
not to resume work until his friends
rebuke him and urge him to return.

Semachot, chap. 9.

It is unlawful for one to enter a
banqueting-house for thirty days after
the death of a relative; but he must
refrain from so doing for twelve months
after the demise of either father or

mother, unless on the behest of some higher requirement of piety.

Semachot, chap. 9.

The After-life, the World to Come and the Days of the Messiah

One wins eternal life after a struggle of years; another finds it in one hour.

Avodah Zarah 17a

All the benedictions in the Temple used to conclude with the words "Blessed be the Lord God of Israel unto eternity;" but when the Sadducees,[23] corrupting the faith, maintained that there was only one world, it was enacted that they should conclude with the words "from eternity unto eternity."

Berakhot 54a

These three will inherit the world to come: — He who dwells in the land of Israel; he who brings up his sons to the study of the Torah; and he who repeats the ritual blessing over the appointed cup of wine at the close of the Sabbath.

Pesachim 113a

There are seven who are not consumed by the worm in the grave, and these are Abraham, Isaac, and Jacob, Moses, Aaron, and Miriam, and Benjamin the son of Jacob.

Bava Batra 17a

All who go down to Gehenna shall come up again, except these three: — He who commits adultery; he who shames another in public; and he who gives another a bad name.

Bava Metzia 58b

A Sadducee once said to Rabbi Abbahu, "Ye say that the souls of the righteous are treasured up under the throne of glory: how then had the Witch of Endor power to bring up the prophet Samuel by necromancy?" The Rabbi replied, "Because that occurred within twelve months after his death; for we are taught that during twelve months after death the body is preserved and the soul soars up and down, but that after twelve months the body is destroyed and the soul goes up never to return."

Shabbat 152b

Elijah said to Rabbi Judah the brother of Rav Salla the Pious, "The world will not last less than eighty-five jubilees, and in the last jubilee the son of David will come."

Sanhedrin 97b

The world is to last six thousand years. Two thousand of these are termed the period of disorder, two thousand belong to the dispensation of the law, and two thousand are the days of the Messiah; but because of our iniquities a large fraction of the latter term is already passed and gone without the Messiah giving any sign of his appearing.

Sanhedrin 97a

Biblical Sidelights

There were ten generations from Adam to Noah, to show how great is God's long-suffering, for each of these went on provoking Him more and more, till His forbearance relenting, He brought the flood upon them.

Avot 5:2

There were ten generations from Noah to Abraham, to show that God is long-suffering, since all those succeeding generations provoked Him, until

Abraham came, and he received the reward that belonged to all of them.

Avot 5:2

"And it came to pass after seven days that the waters of the flood were upon the earth" (Gen. vii. 10). Why this delay of seven days? Rav says they were the days of mourning for Methuselah; and this teaches us that mourning for the righteous will defer a coming calamity. Another explanation is, that the Holy One — blessed be He! — altered the course of nature during these seven days, so that the sun arose in the west and set in the east.

Sanhedrin 108b

Abraham our father had a precious stone suspended from his neck, and every sick person that gazed upon it was immediately healed of his disease. But when Abraham died, God hung up the stone on the sphere of the sun.

Bava Batra 16b

Till Abraham's time there was no such thing as a beard; but as many mistook Abraham for Isaac, and Isaac for Abraham, they looked so exactly alike, Abraham prayed to God for a beard to enable people to distinguish him from his son, Isaac,[24] and it was granted him; as it is written (Gen. xxiv, 1), "And to Abraham a beard came when he was well stricken in age."

Sanhedrin 107b

Rabbi Yehudah says that Abraham planted an ornamental garden with all kinds of choice fruits in it, and Rabbi Nehemiah says that he erected an inn for travelers in order to make known the name of God to all who sojourned in it.

Sotah 10a

On the day when Isaac was weaned, Abraham made a great feast, to which he invited all the people of the land. Not all of those who came to enjoy the feast believed in the alleged occasion of its celebration, for some said contemptuously, "This old couple have adopted a foundling, and provided a feast to persuade us to believe that the child is their own offspring." What did Abraham do? He invited all the great men of the day, and Sarah invited their wives, who brought their infants, but not their nurses, along with them. On this occasion Sarah's breasts became like two fountains, for she supplied, of her own body, nourishment to all the children. Still some were unconvinced, and said, "Shall a child be born to one that is a hundred years old, and shall Sarah, who is ninety years old, bear?" (Gen. xvii. 17.) Whereupon, to silence this objection, Isaac's face was changed, so that it became the very picture of Abraham's; then one and all exclaimed, "Abraham begat Isaac."

Bava Metzia 87a

Abraham our father was tested ten times; in every case he stood firm; which shows how great the love of our father Abraham was.

"And it came to pass after these things that God did test Abraham" (Gen. xxii, 1). After what things? Rabbi Yochanan, in the name of Rabbi Yossi ben Zimra, replies, "After the words of Satan, who said, 'Lord of the Universe! Thou didst bestow a son upon that old man when he was a hundred years of age, and yet he spared not a single dove from the festival to sacrifice to Thee.' God replied, 'Did he not make this festival for the sake of his son? and yet I know he would not refuse to sacrifice that son at my command.' To prove this, God did put Abraham to the test, saying

165

unto him, 'Take now thy son;' just as an earthly king might say to a veteran warrior who had conquered in many a hard-fought battle, 'Fight, I pray thee, this severest battle of all, lest it should be said that thy previous encounters were mere haphazard skirmishes.' Thus did the Holy One — blessed be He! — address Abraham, 'I have tried thee in various ways, and not in vain either; stand this test also, for fear it should be insinuated that the former trials were trivial and therefore easily overcome. Take thy son.' Abraham replied, 'I have two sons.' 'Take thine only son.' Abraham answered, 'Each is the only son of his mother.' 'Take him whom thou lovest.' 'I love both of them,' said Abraham. 'Take Isaac.' Thus Abraham's mind was gradually prepared for this trial. While on the way to carry out this Divine command Satan met him, and (parodying Job iv. 2-5) said, 'Why ought grievous trials to be inflicted upon thee? Behold thou hast instructed many, and thou hast strengthened the weak hands. Thy words have supported him that was falling, and now this sore burden is laid upon thee.' Abraham answered (anticipating Ps. xxvi. 11), 'I will walk in my integrity.' Then said Satan (see Job iv. 6), 'Is not the fear (of God) thy folly? Remember, I pray thee, who ever perished being innocent?' Then finding that he could not persuade him, he said (perverting Job iv. 12), 'Now a word came

to me by stealth. I overheard it behind
the veil (in the Holy of Holies above). A
lamb will be the sacrifice, and not Isaac.'
Abraham said, 'It is the just desert of a
liar not to be believed even when he
speaks the truth.'"

Sanhedrin 89b

"And Esau came from the field, and
he was faint" (Gen. xxv. 29). Rabbi
Yochanan said that wicked man committed on that day five transgressions: —
He committed rape, committed murder,
denied the existence of God, denied the
resurrection of the dead, and despised
the birthright.

Bava Batra 16b

The sons of Esau, of Ishmael, and of Keturah went on purpose to dispute the burial (of Jacob); but when they saw that Joseph had placed his crown upon the coffin, they did the same with theirs. There were thirty-six crowns in all, tradition says. "And they mourned with a great and very sore lamentation." Even the very horses and asses joined in it, we are told. On arriving at the Cave of Machpelah, Esau once more protested, and said, "Adam and Eve, Abraham and Sarah, Isaac and Rebekah, are all buried here. Jacob disposed of his share when he buried Leah in it, and the remaining one belongs to me." "But thou didst sell thy share with thy birthright," remonstrated the sons of Jacob. "Nay," re-

joined Esau, "that did not include my
share in the burial-place." "Indeed it
did," they argued, "for our father, just
before he died, said (Gen. 1.5), 'In my
grave which I have bought for myself.'"
"Where are the title-deeds?" demanded
Esau. "In Egypt," was the answer. And
immediately the swift-footed Naphthali
started for the records.   Hushim, the
son of Dan, being deaf, asked what was
the cause of the commotion. On being
told what it was, he snatched up a club
and smote Esau so hard that his eyes
dropped out and fell upon the feet of
Jacob; at which Jacob opened his eyes
and grimly smiled. This is that which is
written (Ps. lviii. 11), "The righteous
shall rejoice when he sees vengeance; he

shall wash his feet in the blood of the wicked." Then Rebekah's prophecy came to pass (Gen. xxvii. 45), "Why shall I be deprived also of you both in one day?" For although they did not both die on the same day, they were both buried on the same day.

Sotah 13a

The wife of Potiphar coaxed Joseph with loving words, but in vain. She then threatened to immure him in prison, but he replied (anticipating Ps. cxlvi. 7), "The Lord looseth the prisoners." Then she said, "I will bow thee down with distress; I will blind thine eyes." He only answered (*ibid.*, ver. 8), "The Lord openeth the eyes of the blind and raiseth them that are bowed down." She then tried to bribe him with a thousand talents of silver if he would comply with her request, but in vain.

Yoma 35b

Fifty measures of understanding were created in the world, and all except one were given to Moses; as it is said (Ps. viii. 6), "Thou hast made him a little lower than the angels."

Rosh Hashanah 21b

On the seventh of the month Adar, Moses died, and on that day the manna ceased to come down from heaven.

Kiddushin 38a

The seventh of Adar, on which Moses died, was the same day of the same month on which he was born.

Sotah 10b

Seventeen hundred of the arguments and minute rules of the Scribes were forgotten during the days of mourning for Moses. Othniel, the son of Kenaz, by his shrewd arguing restored them all as if they had never lapsed from the memory.

Temurah 16a

Thousands on thousands in Israel were named after Aaron; for had it not been for Aaron these thousands of thousands would not have been born. Aaron went about making peace between quarreling couples, and those who were born after the reconciliation were regularly named after him.

Avot d'Rabbi Nathan 12:4

David had four hundred young men, handsome in appearance and with their hair cut close upon their foreheads, but with long flowing curls behind, who used to ride in chariots of gold at the head of the army. These were men of power, the mighty men of the house of David, who went about to strike terror into the world.

Kiddushin 76b

When Solomon was desirous of conveying the Ark into the Temple, the doors shut themselves of their own accord against him. He cited twenty-four psalms, yet they opened not. In vain he cried, "Lift up your heads, O ye gates" (Ps. xxiv. 9). But when he prayed, "O Lord God, turn not Thy face away from

Thine anointed; remember the mercies of David, thy servant" (II Chron. vi. 42), then the gates flew open at once. Then the enemies of David turned black in the face, for all knew by this that God had pardoned David's transgression with Bathsheba.

Mo'ed Katan 9a

"Now, when Job's three friends heard of all this evil that was come upon him, they came each from his own place; Eliphaz the Temanite, Bildad the Shuhite, and Zophar the Naamathite: for they had made an appointment together to come and mourn with him, and to comfort him" (Job ii, 11). What is meant when it is said, "They had made an appointment together?" Rav Yehudah says in the name of Rav, "This is to teach that they all came in by one gate." But there is a tradition that each lived three hundred miles away from the other. How then came they to know of Job's sad condition? Some say they had wreaths, others say trees (each representing an absent friend), and when any friend was in distress the one representing him straightway began to wither. Rava said, "Hence the proverb, 'Either a friend as the friends of Job, or death.'"

Bava Batra 16b

Rav Yitzchak asks, "Why was Obadiah accounted worthy to be a prophet?" Because, he answers, he concealed a hundred prophets in a cave; as it is said (I Kings xviii. 4), "When Jezebel cut off the prophets of the Lord, Obadiah took a hundred prophets and hid them by fifty in a cave." Why by fifties? Rabbi Eliezer explains, "He copied the plan from Jacob, who said, (Gen. xxxii, 9) 'If Esau come to one company and smite it, then the other company which is left may escape.'" Rabbi Abbahu says, "It was because the caves would not hold any more."

Sanhedrin 39b

"And the inhabitants of Jerusalem did him honor at his death" (II Chron. xxxii. 33). This is Hezekiah, king of Judah, at whose funeral thirty-six thousand people attended bare-shouldered,...and upon his bier was laid a roll of the Torah, and it was said, "This man has fulfilled what is written in this book."

Bava Kama 17a

Glossary

Aggadot — literally, "narrations"; non-legal passages in Rabbinic literature, including philosophical and theological comments, stories, Scriptural interpretations, and observations about health, natural science, and the human condition

Avoda — sacrificial rituals associated with Yom Kippur, the Day of Atonement, during the time of the Temple; recalling the details of that ritual is a major part of the synagogue liturgy on Yom Kippur

Gehenna — originally, Gehinnom, the valley of Hinnom near Jerusalem, where idolatrous rituals were carried out; in Jewish teachings about the after-life, the place where the souls of the wicked are afflicted for a limited interval of time

Gemilut Chasadim — deeds of loving kindness; an all-embracing category of benevolent acts, it includes personal service as well as monetary assistance

Haggadot — see Aggadot

Halachot — laws, legal traditions

Matzot — unleavened bread; eaten on Passover to commemorate the hurried flight of the Israelites from Egypt

Minyan — a quorum of ten adult Jews whose presence is necessary for certain prayers and rituals

Sadducee — member of a faction in the days of the Second Temple that represented the priestly and aristocratic classes; they held to a literal interpretation of Scripture and rejected the Pharisees' belief in the Divine basis of the Oral Torah.

Sanhedrin — supreme religious court; it had legislative as well as judicial powers; ceased to exist with the destruction of the Temple

Shamir — in Rabbinic lore, a mythical worm-like creature that had the ability to eat through stone; its assistance enabled Solomon to build the Temple without violating the prohibition against using stones hewn with an iron implement

Shechinah — the indwelling presence of God

Shema — the passage from Deuteronomy vi.4-9, beginning with the words, "Hear, O Israel, the Lord is our God, the Lord is one"; this prayer, regarded as a recognition and acceptance of God's Sovereignty, is recited twice daily, morning and evening

Torah — the Five Books of Moses, first section of the Hebrew Scriptures; in a broader sense, all Jewish religious teaching; sometimes mistranslated "law", it actually means "teaching"

Tzedakah — literally, "righteousness"; refers to monetary assistance given to the needy

Footnotes

1 Jewish writers, in referring to historical dates, commonly employ the abbreviations BCE (before the Common Era) and CE in preference to the Christian usage of BC and AD.

2 The rabbis derive the principle of deciding the law according to the vote of the majority from a convoluted reading of Exodus xxiii.2 that goes against the plain meaning of the verse. The expression "after a multitude" occurs twice within the verse, implying that when it is "to do evil," one should not follow the majority, but in all other instances the opinion of the majority is to prevail.

3 Although the Scriptures mandate death as the penalty for numerous crimes and offenses and the Talmud itself recognizes capital pun-

ishment as a theoretical possibility, the rabbis, through stringent rules of evidence and procedure, made it almost impossible to sentence a criminal to death.

4 The Hebrew word, *olam*, means both "world" and "everlasting," so the verse from Proverbs can be read, "The righteous man is the foundation of the world."

5 The verse from Ecclesiastes reads, "If the serpent bite before it is charmed, then the charmer hath no advantage." The Hebrew expression here translated "charmer" is literally, "master of language," denoting for the rabbis one who indulges in malicious language, i.e., slander.

6 Maagol means "circle maker," a name given to Choni from his practice of drawing a circle on the ground and standing within it when he prayed for rain. He would vow not to leave the confines of his circle until his prayer was answered.

7 A red heifer was necessary for the rites of purification spelled out in Numbers xix. The

animal was slaughtered and then burned, and its ashes were used in a solution that was sprinkled on those who had contracted ritual impurity through contact with a corpse.

8 The Hebrew term for alms is "tzedakah," literally "righteousness." Benevolence is denoted by "gemilut chasadim," meaning "bestowing of kindnesses."

9 The Hebrew word for "righteousness" is "tzedakah," which also means almsgiving.

10 "Rabbi" refers to Judah ha-Nasi, the redactor of the Mishna.

11 Although sacrificial offerings ceased to be the mode of Jewish worship following the Romans' destruction of the Temple in 70 CE, Rabbinic lore and Jewish liturgy continued to recall the glory of the days when the Temple still stood and to lavish attention on the details of the worship that took place there. For the rabbis, studying about the Temple and the sacrifices was an acceptable substitute for the offerings which could no longer be brought.

12 The wave-sheaf of the new barley crop was brought as an offering in conjunction with the observance of Passover (the precise time for this offering was a matter of dispute). Two wave-loaves were baked from the newly-harvested wheat and were offered on the holiday of Shavuot, seven weeks after Passover. The shew-bread consisted of twelve loaves displayed on a table in the inner sanctuary of the Temple and replaced weekly on the eve of the Sabbath.

13 The first paragraph of this selection is the opening section of the Mishna. The following paragraphs are the Gemara's discussion of the text.

Those of priestly descent (kohanim) were supported by a special tax on the produce of the people known as the terumah or heave-offering (something that is "lifted up"). The offering could only be eaten by one who was in a state of ritual purity.

14 The word "congregation" ("edah" in Hebrew) is defined in Rabbinic tradition as ten adults, the "minyan" or quorum neces-

sary before certain prayers can be said. In Genesis xviii, God was willing to pardon the people of Sodom and Gomorrah, if a minimum of ten righteous people could be found. In Numbers xiv, the ten scouts who brought back a negative report about the land of Canaan are referred to as an "evil congregation."

15 Shimon and his son were in the cave hiding from the Roman authorities.

16 There are two different versions of the Ten Commandments in the Torah. "Remember" in the Exodus version is interpreted by the rabbis to refer to such things as special food and clothing by which we honor the Sabbath. "Keep" in Deuteronomy refers to refraining from forbidden labor on the Sabbath day.

17 This is a description of the preparations for the Avoda, the ritual of Yom Kippur, the Day of Atonement, that was carried out in the time of the Temple. The High Priest would enter the Holy of Holies and cleanse it from the accumulated transgressions of the people. The Avoda entailed sacrificial offerings, con-

fession of sins, and the symbolic riddance of
the people's sins, which were transferred to
a goat that was banished to the wilderness.
Though these rituals have not been practiced
since the destruction of the Temple, a dra-
matic description of the Avoda, recalling the
days of the Temple, is a centerpiece of the
synagogue liturgy for Yom Kippur.

18 Chanuka commemorates the victorious
struggle of the Jews (168-165 BCE) against
the Seleucid king, Antiochus IV, who attempted to stamp out the practice of the
Jewish religion. Though based in Syria, the
Seleucid monarchy was one of the successors
to the empire of Alexander the Great and was
devoted to the promotion and spread of Greek
culture. Chanuka means "dedication" and
celebrates the rededication of the Temple to
the worship of God. The practice recom-
mended by the school of Hillel, of lighting an
additional candle on each of the successive
nights of Chanuka, is now the established
custom.

19 The ninth of Av (which occurs during the summer of the year) is a fast and a day of mourning, recalling both the destruction of the First Temple by the Babylonians in 586 BCE and the Second Temple by the Romans in 70 CE.

20 The text of Exodus xxiv.7 is translated "we will do and we will obey," but the Hebrew word for "obey" can also be translated "hear." The rabbis attributed to the Israelites a willingness to fulfill God's commandment, even before they had heard what it entailed. The sin referred to in this passage is the worship of the Golden Calf.

21 The words "from Bashan," if vocalized differently in Hebrew, can be read "from with the tooth."

22 Rabbi the Holy refers to Judah ha-Nasi, the redactor of the Mishna.

23 The word "olam" in Hebrew means both "world" and "eternity." The words "from eternity to eternity" could also be read "from world to world" and would hint at the exist-

ence of a world other than our present one, thus affirming the possibility of an afterlife. The Sadducees, being literalists, rejected such Pharasaic doctrines as the world to come and the resurrection of the dead, because they could find no Scriptural warrant for these concepts.

24 The text literally says, "And Abraham was old, advanced in age." The rabbis' fanciful interpretation is made possible by the similarity of the word for "old" ("zaken") and the word for "beard" ("zakan").